COACHES

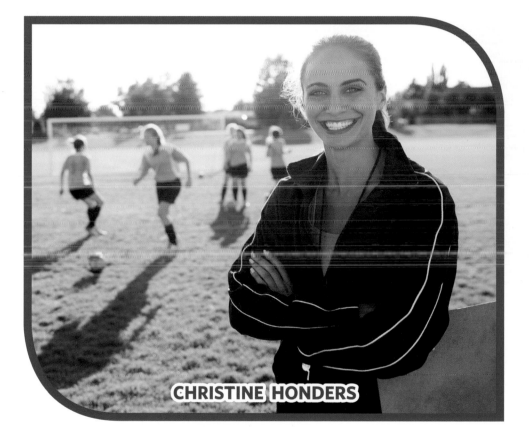

CHRISTINE HONDERS

PowerKiDS
press™

New York

Published in 2020 by The Rosen Publishing Group, Inc.
29 East 21st Street, New York, NY 10010

First Edition

Editor: Greg Roza
Book Design: Reann Nye

Photo Credits: Cover, p.1 Hero Images/Getty Images; pp. 4–22 Abstractor/Shutterstock.com; pp. 5, 15 Thomas Barwick/DigitalVision/Getty Images; pp. 7, 19 Monkey Business Images/Shutterstock.com; p. 9 Microgen/Shutterstock.com; p. 11 Jose Luis Pelaez Inc/DigitalVision/Getty Images; p. 13 Lucky Business/Shutterstock.com; p. 17 Alistair Berg/DigitalVision/Getty Images; p. 21 Fuse/Corbis/Getty Images; p. 22 sirtravelalot/Shutterstock.com.

Library of Congress Cataloging-in-Publication Data

Names: Honders, Christine author.
Title: Coaches / Christine Honders.
Description: New York : PowerKids Press, [2020] | Series: Helpers in our
   community | Includes webography. | Includes index.
Identifiers: LCCN 2019011608| ISBN 9781725308145 (paperback) | ISBN
   9781725308169 (library bound) | ISBN 9781725308152 (6 pack)
Subjects: LCSH: Coaches (Athletics)–Juvenile literature.
Classification: LCC GV711 .H646 2020 | DDC 796.07/7–dc23
LC record available at https://lccn.loc.gov/2019011608

Manufactured in the United States of America

CPSIA Compliance Information: Batch #CWPK20. For Further Information contact Rosen Publishing, New York, New York at 1-800-237-9932.

CONTENTS

Sports in America

People all over the world watch and play sports. In the United States, it's a big part of our **culture**. You may have a team you like best. Maybe you play a sport. There's one thing that all sports teams have in common. They all have a coach.

Does a Team Need a Coach?

Even the best players need a leader. If a team didn't have a coach, they might not know what to do. Coaches teach them the skills they need. They come up with plans to win. Coaches help players work together to become a great team.

Reaching Your Goals

Coaches help **athletes** figure out what they're best at. They watch them play and help them improve their skills. Coaches make sure players stay healthy. They help athletes reach their goals of being the best they can be!

Teachers and Trainers

Coaches teach the rules of the sport. They train athletes to help them get better. Coaches plan exercises to help players learn skills such as throwing or catching. They may have practice games to **encourage** players to work together as a team.

Ready to Win

Coaches want their team to win! They watch games or meets closely and tell athletes what to do next. Coaches may change a team's plan in the middle of a game. They also study the other team's **strategies** and try to figure out how to beat them.

More Than a Coach

Coaching isn't just about teaching. Good coaches **motivate** their players. They create a fun **environment** so the players learn a love for the game. They give each player the help and support they need. Good coaches may be almost like family.

Good Sportsmanship

A good coach has good sportsmanship. This means they treat other coaches and players with respect. Coaches shake hands after a game to show good sportsmanship. They make sure their players don't tease other players or argue with the other team.

Becoming a Coach

Most coaches were once athletes in their sport. Many coaches work at schools. Coaches at high schools and colleges are often teachers. Some take classes about sports science and safety. But you don't have to go to college to coach a community team.

Professional Teams

Professional sports teams need professional coaches. "Professional" means they're paid to play or coach. Professional teams may have many coaches. They have coaches who give attention to different skills. Some coaches travel to high schools and colleges, looking for new players.

Coaching Life Lessons

Good coaches teach life lessons. They show us our strengths and how to become even stronger. They encourage us to work together. They help us when things get tough. Coaches show us that hard work and teamwork will help us win in life!

GLOSSARY

athlete: Someone who is trained in or good at sports.

culture: The beliefs and ways of life of a certain group of people.

encourage: To make someone more hopeful or determined.

environment: Everything that is around a person.

motivate: To give a reason for doing something.

strategy: A plan of action to achieve a goal.

INDEX

WEBSITES

Due to the changing nature of Internet links, PowerKids Press has developed an online list of websites related to the subject of this book. This site is updated regularly. Please use this link to access the list: www.powerkidslinks.com/HIOC/coaches